Fearn

Linda Dove

Fearn

Cooper
Dillon

Acknowledgments

I am ever grateful to the editors and readers of the following publications, where the poems listed first appeared, sometimes in different form:

Cease, Cows: "Fear Is a Walk through Immovable Trees"
Coffin Bell Journal: "Fear Is a Bucket by the Rainspout"
Interim: A Journal of Poetry and Poetics: "Fear Is a Paper-Trail Inside Your Body"
Passager: "Fear Is a Mullioned Window Inside a Rabbit's Eye"
Phantom Drift Limited: "Fear Is a Stick-Figure Made of Wood" and "Fear Is a Bird-Verb like To Parrot"
Rattle: "Fear Is the Day that Isn't Ordinary"

Fearn
Copyright © 2019 by Linda Dove
All rights reserved. First edition.

Cooper Dillon Books
San Diego, California
CooperDillon.com

Cover Image: Panel 15 from *the ocean is an archive, the ocean has no memory* by Elizabeth Dove. elizabethdove.com

Book Design: Adam Deutsch

ISBN-13: 978-1943899-09-8

Table of Contents

Fear Is the Key to Every Map, Every Eye	3
Fear Is a Stick-Figure Made of Wood	4
Fear Is a Ballot Box Colonized like a Hive	5
Fear Is a Paper-Trail Inside Your Body	7
Fear Is the Street-Fair Animal's Eye	8
Fear Is a Walk through Immovable Trees	9
Fear Is a Hummingbird Drunk on Taillight	11
Fear Is a Bucket by the Rainspout	12
Fear Is a Fortune Cookie after Dreaming	13
Fear Is a Bird-Verb like To Parrot	14
Fear Is a Calendar Seen in a Flower	16
Fear Is Dreaming What Waves Dream	17
Fear Is a New Monster, Half-Mother	19
Fear Is a World's Departure from a Hinge	20
Fear Is the Day that Isn't Ordinary	21
Fear Is a Love Letter to Beethoven's Missing Waltz	22
Fear Is a Sky that Moves Away from Us	23
Fear Is a Field of Poppies Blossoming, Then Blown	24
Fear Is the Mockingbird That Sings All Night Long	25
Fear Is a Fence of Trees Seen from a Field	26
Fear Is a Room with a View to the Sea	28
Fear Is That the Dead Know Everything About You Now	29
Fear Is a Standard Candle in Space	30
Fear Is the Voyager That Will Outlive the Earth	31
Fear Is the Creep of Body away from You	32
Fear Is a Mullioned Window Inside a Rabbit's Eye	33
Fear Is Learning Your Best Exit May Be Behind You	34
Fear Is an Envoi to the Future	36

The apple was fear.
—Mary Ruefle

Fear Is the Key to Every Map, Every Eye
> *See how the one you turn from*
> *turns out to be what will not let you go.*
>   *—Catherine Abbey Hodges*

It always starts with fear. Isn't that what is
at the bottom of every well, which is a story

told with water but is really about the rope-
puller or the face in the skim of the bucket.

The body always begins with a short object.
A gun or a bird. Perhaps an idea. It

is always changing its shape, covering
for spilled sins like a Persian carpet

with a thick pile of pink and blue fur. It
substitutes one thing for another, one fear

for a coin, one fear for a fern, one for an
unburned house. You can't see the eye

of the polar bear from where you're standing
because it looks like a stone in the snow. It

is safer to look at fear in a box, to pull fox-
gloves over your hands like suits of petals.

Fear Is a Stick-Figure Made of Wood

It hangs out with trees
because it's hard to escape where it comes from.
It is looking at you,
the human, the heart
on the sleeve.
It doesn't use clothes as cover
because it has no use for charm.
At night, it is the legs on your bed.
In the day, it's the splinter in your thumb
that means you don't forget skin.
It doesn't let you forget.
Not totally.
It makes a brokenness
that doesn't know what to do with itself.
It is not just wood-bogged thumbs
anymore, it is eyes where tiny canoes live.
Not surprisingly,
it thinks of itself as potential.
It is skinny and liable to snap
in two like matches that line up
for their chance to burn.

Fear Is a Ballot Box Colonized like a Hive

It is never just about making your mark,
black dots trooping down a voting card

like ants. What does it mean, the most good
for the most? We dip in and out of priorities.

Now it's the President flirting with evil.
Now it's my father falling in the kitchen,

his head wedged under the cabinet
and blood pooling. Now it's the wasps

building a comb in the window well.
The clouds are still lavender at dawn.

This poem could turn pastoral
at any moment, given its provenance.

Why do we speak of casting our ballot,
as if we're losing our line to the current

or playing a game of marbles? We used to
vote with round stones, which explains our pebble

government. Invasion is the lesser form
of desire, but what you actually need

is almost nothing. If you've ever fled
a house, you know. To rescue anything

beautiful is just dumb luck and a crack
because holes beg for meaning. What's the point

of a queen if a broom handle keeps knocking
the nest away? They start again in the morning,

inventing their lives from scratch,
making a home with their mouths.

Fear Is a Paper-Trail Inside Your Body

It is a map to a place you once knew, a college town, a park made of oak trees and woodpeckers, the rented rooms in California. The map has become second-nature and familiar, like an organ of the body. In the house, you don't think about where you're going, you just move down hallways and through doors. You can still see the campus in your mind, the copper beech, the way feet have worn small bowls in the marble of the library steps. You are intimate with the order of it. Its orientation in you in space.

The map is more like a machine than a piece of paper. You think maybe it should slip away, as memories do. It does not. It keeps running its program behind your eyes. It leads you without much mental effort. Years later, you can put one foot in front of the other while doing something else—talking on the phone, for instance, or looking at the sky—and arrive at the field of bobolinks, even if the bobolinks aren't there anymore. But chances are they are—squeaking and crinking like digital birds, and the trail inside your body still works.

It is unnerving, this news that there are runways inside you, with engines taking off. Organs flying at cruising altitude all night long, over the Pacific, while you try to sleep. You spend years not paying attention to the way your heart beats, or even that it beats. But then, when you try to recall specifically what it feels like—to run with it, to hike the canyon with it, to love with it humming and racing up and down in tune to what your body demands of it, to sit in the dark with it, all alone—you can't remember it, not precisely. Just the idea of it having been. The way a map is not the land itself, but a representation. The way a heartbeat is not the organ, but the organ speaking.

Fear Is the Street-Fair Animal's Eye

> *The camels stand in all their vague beauty—*
> *at night they fold up like pale accordions.*
>   —Rita Dove

It happens over the heads of children.
It is his eyelashes surrounding
each brown bulb. It is his camel toe,
which he pulls up into himself as he looks.
It is the itch. What do I think
he thinks? He who stands like a church
at the corner, pacing the hard pavement
when there's a dune hanging
by a thread in his eye. His handlers
are laughing under his chin.
He stares across them. The children
play him like an instrument. He sounds
like their dreams except holy,
how you might store toys in a sanctuary
or a sepulchre. He hums a hymn
through a space that has never heard it
before—the guts of a tin whistle,
a tambourine, an accordion.
He displaces the desire for ponies.
The crowd holds its breath
at his otherness. He flashes back
our need to own the strangeness
in his eye by riding him around
the usual circle. It is similar
to the displacement caused by a coin
tossed in a pool, when, somewhere
near the edge, a token of water
splashes out, offset by the tithe.

Fear Is a Walk through Immovable Trees
at the botanic garden, Claremont, California

It is the wolf
with the yellow wing
in its eye. No.
It is more like a blister of sap,
pinecones blown across
the garden. In the grove,
the oaks don't lose their leaves
and can't be moved by law.
Instead, it turns its attention
to the brevifolia, the brief leaves
of the Joshua Trees
that bend to the ground like we do
to read the signs—or, maybe,
like time does. Time is relative
here. It has no use for us.
It will turn down our words,
having others. In this fairytale
garden, it reminds us
of the fairytale child
we almost had. She was going
before she arrived, when
we would have named her
after a tree—
Rowan,
Willow,
Fern.
She is the ghost
we might see in the water
if we pass by a pool,
where we might want
to assume a bottom

since some depths echo
the unstarred sky.
But back to the wolf,
visiting today in the gardens,
standing at the edge of everything—
like the wolf, it is always
a matter of degree.
It is the paws staked in the dirt,
and the snow-blind coat,
and also the eye
that moves under water like a gold coin.

Fear Is a Hummingbird Drunk on Taillight

Red is the operative word.
Its throat glows
in its own accusative tense.
It spears the red tails
of your car in the turn lane.
It thinks you are flowers,
the kind that bloom at night
and in rain with fierce, electric
petals. It is out of control.
It will do anything.
It hunts the light caught
in boxes—the blinkers,
the voice. More often,
you are silent
in the face of it.
It is so tiny—
a miniature version
of you that can also
fly backwards.
It thinks it knows
your organs: the heart's
one rule
that breaks all the others.

Fear Is a Bucket by the Rainspout

It sits empty without weather. It learns
to wait, its metal a hole of slack.
Then it storms, and
it fills.
The sound gusts through
every odd chance.
To answer it, you find whatever words
that you must say out loud—
or die—
because the bucket has put them in you.
It turns its glare soft with water,
the blue of something big on its surface.
Its clouds, its birds, are brief.
They are tricks of the eye.
The dead bee
is real, a vain floater.
The pail holds this pollen-bit speck
against sky and damps
the buzz.
Somewhere a dance.
Somewhere soon a darkening,
moonlight
that falls on the day's accident
and strips the sodden wings
to tongues.

Fear Is a Fortune Cookie after Dreaming

It is the tongue of paper reading *Prepare for difficulties
if you dream of salt*. You have just been to sleep

in a mineral blizzard, where the flakes stormed and spouted
from the sidewalk through blowholes and fell back to earth

like fountains. People carried umbrellas. It was a concrete blur,
not like the Morton's salt girl at all: *when it rains it pours,*

she skipped, which is another way to say, prepare for
difficulties, though the marketing campaign tells you

that salt is as easy as water, that girls dress in yellow
and dance through the drops, that your kitchen can withstand

the coming storm, as if the floor you are walking on
won't suddenly burst open with difficult rain.

Fear Is a Bird-Verb like To Parrot

It is the quick sleight of beak replacing lip, like a purse clasp that clicks shut on a clutch of coins. It has a need to keep things from you.

It roosts in a large tree but not like a cartoon vulture because it is green with wings that might be leaves. Every stem is a small branch.

It appears new that way. It looks relevant in its coat of green, which does not stand for envy in this poem but maybe something more like survival.

It is a parrot that parrots. It prefers to reproduce itself, to collapse its lavender feathers like a folded fan. It wants you to turn your nouns into verbs

so that your tongue is a bannister held by a firm hand. It is hard to see what-is-what. It is quick. It takes away its chucks and whistles and hob-nobs

all at once in a sky slurry, which means there is a flock that lifts off in unison or close to it. Nothing is as it seems against a backdrop of blue. It puts you on defense or on-guard or in-a-nutshell because you are left on the ground, staring up at its escape on a wing and a prayer, except you are the one

who's praying now. It hands you the verbs you need—*to parrot*, of course, but also, *to swallow*, *to crow*, *to duck*. It wants you to believe that letters are not

in full molt, but then it adds *to owl* and *to egret*. And this is where language starts to fail you. Its words get quiet in the dark like animals

when they sit on a branch under a branch and wait for the light or like ocean in the trough of a wave. Across a fetch of open water, it is both a bird

and a verb, such as *to tern*. On land, it is a thing that thrives among the trees, *to nuthatch* down, *to creeper* up, where even *bark* sounds an alarm

out of a feral parrot that once lived with a dog. Now you take yourself off the hook of language that wrote you into the forest as an oracle

because you are not an oracle, though you lie down on the forest floor. In the morning inside the tree inside you is an unmade staircase.

15

Fear Is a Calendar Seen in a Flower
fireweed, Alaska

It pinks the spaces,
time-stalking.
You turn aware
that this green moment
moves.
It disappears
from the bottom up,
which makes it possible
to read the season in a flower,
as if you could stamp
a sell-by date
on summer.
In this way, it burns
itself out.
Behind it,
underneath,
sticks pile up
on the stem,
like little windows
lacking glass.
It turns against
its regular beauty,
the kind that blushes
whole fields,
offering instead
a grid,
tiny muntins
that mean your eye
will not fall
unbound
into that largeness.

Fear Is Dreaming What Waves Dream

It is a problem of similarities. One flap of ocean folds harshly
over another, the way I snap

the sheets to fit above an unmade bed. Water curls and wedges
into itself, pushes the future

forward, sand settling like the parts of a life that can be changed.
There is a date (it's 3-31-12

if you must know) that splits the world, water from earth, sea from
sky, not like when the horizon line

disappears and the color-blocks bleed into a single gray screen,
the offing somewhere in the near

distance, unreadable but unmistakeble. My life turns into a trick
of being told what the next word is

or when to speak the anger or what. Some language looks like
other language. I can't speak

and survive. I can't name the way out of this crude cutting-off,
when safe becomes not-safe

and home is a dark tentacle. When two words are too
close, their dreams enter each

other. Water is a mirror. Past the breakers. In a trough. Where
I'm carried by the swell

the way leaves carry on the wind, all the linden trees lined up
in the park, in the preserve,

a small sea of squirrels and foxes and birds that have briefly
stopped using their wings.

Signs warn me not to feed the animals. The waves of wind
dream of the signs, dream

the animals are not real, the date is not real, the ocean can be
sucked back into itself. The ocean

dreams of itself. Its insistence on replicating its form, over and
over, on carrying me out

to sea with the news that rip tides aren't real. It wants me to drown
in its spin and tumble. It wants me

to dream the waves are trees, the sand is snow piling in drifts.
Its invention of itself depends on my belief

that the ocean is also a house, is also a school, is also a shop, a car,
a dog, a laptop, a recipe, a phone. The ocean

is the ocean and not the ocean. It says. The ocean is a forest, where
I can measure the space between fake bears.

Fear Is a New Monster, Half-Mother

It frankensteins you forever. You leave
the marriage or he does. The result is
you are now a new creature, only half
a mother to your daughter. She tutors
you in the new language of *your house*
and *not-your-house*, so that when she leaves,
she is *not-your-daughter*. You wait for her
to return. It doesn't turn to winter but it is
so hot that you regret the need to breathe.
You indulge this threat. In the mirror,
you see the mother-half with the glossy
new skin like citrus, a luna moth drinking
from your ear. It is your better side
for photographs. The other half contracts
so far into a point, it disappears.
The joke about how it's not possible
to be a little pregnant, you get it,
you who are a little bit of mother.
You know your daughter says she likes
the arrangement—she never gets bored.
Half the time, you don't believe her.
Her life goes by in half the time, too,
for you. Your loss is never complete,
a thought you immediately wish back.
You feel guilty for the suggestion
that you are never not her mother,
and—let's be real—guilty for mourning
a loss that hasn't killed her.
Her laughter is unchoked by dirt.
She will sometimes arrive at *your house*
in jeans you haven't bought her,
roses running down the seams,
all legs and thread and patchwork.

Fear Is a World's Departure from a Hinge
based on a line from Emily Dickinson

It was a soul-scene, a landscape hinged to me
by the fact that I had memorized the rocks.
When you memorize something, you take it
for your companion animal, your familiar,
your everlasting luck. It was meant to be
my last act, my ashes stuck in the granite dirt
near the bones of my dogs and the wild larkspur.
It wasn't minor. I miss it like I miss the world
when it betrays me, when it takes something away
that I thought I should have forever. I prefer salt
to sweet, which is another way to love
the earth. It made me care about my dead body.
How's that for superlatives? The sun goes extinct
every night there by disappearing into the rocks,
which hold the heat against the dark
so that it can find itself again, like a bank vault
or a mother's wrist you grab on the way
down. There is a stone there the color of peaches
and cream, long and flat, near the top
of the main trail, and you should know that
it is beautiful. When I let go, I thought of it—
the way it knew me once and now it doesn't.

Fear Is the Day that Isn't Ordinary

It is not the alarm clock and the coffee
and the work. It is not this morning,
when I read poems and had time
to shave the hair growing from the backs
of my knees. For a long time, I watched
a sparrow shoveling water out of the birdbath,
using his bill like the bucket of a bulldozer.
I ate apples I pulled from the tree.
This morning I watched the news. I saw
the kennels we've built to hold the others—
the children and the mothers and the fathers—
and I know that I can decide I don't want to
travel, which is another way to lose.
I can afford to stay in one place. It is a luxury
to call a home home. To see your name
on a gravestone. To know the local words
for *first light* and *water* and *help*.
To look at the apple's skin and not see
a map or a shroud. I know where I belong
at least some of the time. I know there is a jar
parked on a mountain high above the border
between Arizona and Mexico. It holds
notes—the voices of hikers and star-gazers
who followed a canyon wren off the trail.
It is full of the ordinary past—weather,
dates, names. Nothing special, nothing
like what those bodies hold, crossing
below it. Sometimes, on an ordinary day,
I think of the fact of it, hovering over the desert
like its own country, those dispersals
casually trusted to the earth, the way we offer
bits of ourselves to the air when we sing.

Fear Is a Love Letter to Beethoven's Missing Waltz

It is waking up with me
with you
with words in my head.
It is sometimes the rain
at the window.
The rain makes everything different
that is the same.
It makes its little adjustments
to the sky
and the streets
and your hands that are suddenly wet
because they try to be an umbrella,
something they're not.
You are not a love letter, either,
or a dance
or a composer who has lost
his hearing, although I too
am scared of sound
retreating, like your voice
at the departures gate
or when you read this poem.
It is wrong
to say you are one thing
standing in for another
even if you share certain qualities
with the rain,
the way it breaks apart
on the sill.
When I look at a single lens,
I see the world, blue
your eye.

Fear Is a Sky that Moves Away from Us
based on a photograph of Grand Teton National Park

It is not still, so it is not
the fence of mountains.
Overhead, the clouds blear
like whitewater
and make a whole world
on the other side of this one.
It moves like it is being chased
or maybe pulled or like there is some
sort of reel-to-reel
with an up-tempo soundtrack
that animates the sky
but not the ground.
It is the jagged seam between
before and after.
At any time, it may unzip
and spill all that isn't
gone. It will open
to the place
inside the place
where we live.
Of course, the clouds do not return.
The peaks flatten to panels
on a stage, which we skim
on our way to the backdrop
with the impossible blur.
What happens now
is a tarantella that begins
off-stage, on four strings.
Inside the clouds
is the violin and inside the violin,
a room, a door.

Fear Is a Field of Poppies Blossoming, Then Blown
after a line by James Longenbach

It pays to study the way flowers behave,
their tendency to fledge and fall
like birds, their pointed undressing.
To open was the point, after all.
It is important to *expect the unexpected,*
to *remain available to what comes.*
After all the hell of snow,
it melted and didn't change much.
Or everything was different.
It is hard to tell since we have
come to believe in the promise
of petals. Trust may be a green chain
ready to give, a late spring,
a season we thought we knew.
We turn to words like *sweetie*
and *honey* because habit is a help
in uncertain weather. We let
the bright blossoms wave in us.
We let the ground feel like ground.
We walk on it. We walk up mountains
to prove we can defy forward motion.
The opening eventually peels past
some tipping point, the poppies
stretch the bounds of blooming.
After petalfall, the air is piked
by stems. *Darling*, we say
in a field spread with small blankets.

Fear Is the Mockingbird That Sings All Night Long

It is outside while we talk
in the room of windows
somewhere
in a tree or on a line
telling the dark it doesn't mind
the dark. It is insisting
that it could go on.
It cannot know, cannot know
it will wake up on a day
far from this one
and praise the bleak rim of sun
for what it is.
Morning is no precept.
How long until it knows
that daybreak is
like heartbreak is
like breakfast,
a petty violence?
The bird sings
against the words, over
and over, demanding
we allow for the idea
that sound survives,
even though
this conversation will not
change minds. All of us
are stubborn in our own ways,
in our gray suits.

Fear Is a Fence of Trees Seen from a Field
> *And all the lives we ever lived and all the lives to be*
> *are full of trees and changing leaves.*
>   *—Virginia Woolf*

It holds our bodies open like bags stuffed with raked leaves.
Our lives are full of trees because we dream in forests,

because trees are what we breathe, the first lollipop-shape
we crayon. We live many lives, not just one green bloom,

except for those evergreens, ever-impressed with a single
look. I see that I am middle-aged, more than half-way

done. As I broom the leafmeal, I am counting deaths,
a leaf, a leaf. Each jagged reach that's torn or crushed.

Each stem. Each perfect specimen that drops red
and flat to the ground. This year my hair stopped mixing

salt with pepper and silvered like the sides of fish.
When a storm is coming, the undersides of leaves turn

to mirrors. I could have stayed. I could have kept one
or an other of another life, made a go of it, said no to what

the wind wanted. I didn't trust accumulation, so I traded
lakes for deserts and deserts for cities and rooms for rooms.

The seasons of dogs straddle ours, the lives I've pressed
shut in heavy books. Their fur survives the falling stars

of trees, which smudge the pages brown. Now I read
words through the vein of a broken window, an EKG.

It's nostalgia that comes when we call. It pants at our feet, fetches a prettier word than regret. Fetches branches.

Branches. Swizzle sticks of chance. At forest's edge is a line between trees and not-trees. The world begins there.

Fear Is a Room with a View to the Sea

It welts the skyline with red fireworks
as I sit on your couch and sip prosecco

and play your game of subsitution, where I
tell you a yellow bird is a sparrow. The bubbles

rise in the glass like tiny flares. You want
to gossip, you want to stare regret in the face

without apology. You were probably the one.
In the desert, I learned to love you

by naming each grain of sand. But you kept
searching for the sweat lodge

fogged with smoke, the canyon
that flooded. You were always walking

into stories. I have learned to listen
because pity and desire

both mix in the bowl of survival. I don't
know how to stop folding you in,

pushing the air into dough, squaring
laundry. Even the daily chores tie me

to the need for you. You feed me
what you want, and I turn tipsy

from wanting to rise to the top. This is not
the same thing as wanting to win.

Fear Is that the Dead Know Everything About You Now

It is the lilac, planted in defiance in the desert.
        It's not that the tree doesn't bud in the heat,
           but that the leaves—bold and heart-shaped—transform it

overnight into a green dress. So flowers can be petalless
        and haunted. Unidentifiable as flowers.
           The lilacs are like lies that only the dead

can see. Your dead parents see past the leaf-bolt
        to the purple tongues or the blowsy white breath.
           It is impossible to hide your skill with lilacking

from them, even though they will not be horrified.
        They are resigned to understanding. But you smell
           the horror on you, a corpse or two away

from the graveyard. It is satisfying to think that some vases
        won't hold flowers. It is almost enough.
           It is as though your dead grandmother can do the work

of the living, hear the dirt speak, so many roots confessing
        their need for drink. Sometimes this is all that's left.
           Justice built in the sky. *The shred, the shred.*

The blight. The blear. This world is not made to be an orchard,
        to pay as you pick. You must accept your tree
           of chaotic bouquets: all those shades of lavender

and blue, spilling over truth's salty lip. Nothing-petals.
        This lilac belongs to the ghosts
           of bees. They will find it sweet.

Fear Is a Standard Candle in Space

It lands at the door estranged. It knows no one, not the Joshua
trees, not one skin it darkens.

>   I look at my daughter.
>   She has no idea what I've done.

Maybe there's no such thing as a fresh start since the light
we live in arrives old.

>   I change out purses, moving lipsticks
>   and kleenex from space to space. Fortunes.

Light shows me the space between two bodies. What we measure
is not a star, but the distance from name to name.

>   We're all Facebook friends, despite how we stretch
>   our lives like the galaxy's long arms.

Mostly I just lose sight of the sky, the mountains and their far side,
covered in conifers and rain.

>   This is the real ancient trick: the light comes back
>   like a dog with the sun in its mouth.

Fear Is the Voyager That Will Outlive the Earth
> *The Voyager message is carried by a phonograph record...*
> *containing sounds and images selected to portray*
> *the diversity of life and culture on Earth.*
> *—NASA (1977)*

It is stuck to a gold record that pinpoints us
in space, a dot a length or so away from this
or that pulsar, a map none of us can read.

When we are gone—and I don't mean dead,
I mean obliterated by the sun bursting like a grape
between teeth—when all the fossils of all

the bones of all the meat and muscle and skin
that ever moved and are now dust filter out
into their star-grave, when the bottom of the

Mariana Trench meets its black match—
what will survive of us is an hour. It will be
skimming the vacuum without power, humming

the alone tune, missing its signal back for so long
that it will have forgotten it was made.
All evidence of its gods turned flotsam now.

In fact, there is no "now." There is no "here."
Dark Was the Night, Cold Was the Ground
will ache across the space that Blind Willie

Johnson saw coming. When all of us are gone
like we never were, the whales will sing
with whatever meaning they've always meant.

Fear Is the Creep of Body away from You

It knows itself when it sees it. It is the outline
of a dead body that is made up of outlines
of other dead bodies because chalk is ancient
skeletons. Even though I know I breathe closer
to dying every day, it is surprising to learn
all that my body contains. It makes me suspect
it, that it is hiding news from me, plotting,
so that even while I sleep, creatures chew
the marrow of the house around me. I can hang
all the pretty pictures I want on the walls
as they mutate, making new rooms I can't see.
When the radiologist showed me
the calcifications on film, they were
like reverse shadows—white quilling inside
the gray shape of breast. The cancer followed
my milk ducts instead of clumping, a thin
reach of antlers. A rack in my rack.
I cut it all out. I gave away some body parts,
which felt like contrition but also
like tossing beads at Mardi Gras, over
and over, as fast as you can, away, away
to all those grabbing hands. I couldn't
get rid of it quick enough, and now
it haunts me, my deer haint, my doe.
Between the lath in the ribs of the house,
she paces and misses her milk teeth.
She wanders the rooms with her flattened
skin, searching for sheds on the wall.

Fear Is a Mullioned Window Inside a Rabbit's Eye
after Albrecht Dürer (1502)

It is the mullions that give pause. Otherwise,
it is just a square of light, a glint of paint
meant to quicken the hare. But the cross-
pieces—the transom—bring the room into the room.
The rabbit is a wall we are looking through.
That afternoon, there were clouds in Nuremburg,
and it's true that weather can tell time,
caught inside the window inside the eye.
It can divide us, the way the crossbars of wood
split glass. Once, there was a blizzard
that shut the cities for days. I was twelve.
We had to walk out of our streets to bigger streets
the plows could reach. We had to cut paths
—trenches—through the thigh-high snow,
criss-crossing each other's errands.
Babies come in this sort of weather.
They don't pay attention to the reports
and come in search of milk and air.
Bodies leave in this weather, too,
just doing what they want, every hair bent
to every breeze, leaning into the time
when fields dried gold ready to make a fire
like the fur of this rabbit, whose eye is a steady pane
and perhaps more of a shop window
through which we might gaze in on cakes
or sapphires or millinery feathers
rather than out on snow. In this weather
it's hard to know which side of the rabbit
we're on, whether the light catches the silver
knife and the fruits on the table near us,
or whether it skips out along the road-
in-the-eye to places we can't see.

Fear Is Learning Your Best Exit May Be Behind You

It is not an airplane that falters in the sky
or the bag of air that opens like grace.
You aren't in economy, half-listening
to an explanation of what to do
when this day becomes the worst day.

Instead, you have landed on the calendar
where it meant something, 25 years ago.
You imagine the anniversary party
you are missing in that other life.
You imagine it like a lost fish,

a hook. You stand near the shoreline
holding a piece of bent metal, your feet
in a green current. You glance over
your shoulder at dry land, the escape
to a different summer that resembles

a picnic of whatever food is inevitable.
Back there, under the desert willow,
all the doors flap apart ahead of you,
your mouth is an ungashed gill.
Your body still not open to the air.

There, too, is a dog you buried
in the ochre dirt of Arizona, which is
a grave you always thought you'd have,
as if we can own the dead. You thought
you could keep 60 acres of salt

bush and creosote—the oldest living
thing—and each flecked skin of granite that you
knew by heart. But we don't keep. We curate.
It has to be enough that a hillside
will possess those gods and clocks and trails

as much as the penstemon or the fish
that flash through the canyon.
You will think of them on the last day,
when your exits hang like a display
of lures and reels from some wall.

Fear Is an Envoi to the Future

> *People don't live long enough*
> *to see the end*
> *of their experiments.*
>   —*Eloise Klein Healy*

It lingers—

in the upstairs room, the hitch of cannonballs to bed.

    The unhinged legs.

My father, who is dying, can't walk across the artillery
range he imagines, the neurons misfiring, his buried mines
and mortars.

His past is an explosion.

                          Where are the days?

    I move up, into place. I'm next.

I hope my objects forgive me.

                          Who will talk to the
                          candlesticks?

                          Who will finger the
                          gilt and green edges?

The remains of the grandmothers will scatter, crystal
tumblers cut with daisies lost to the copper bellows.

Counting in dogs, I'll have two more lives, perhaps three, if
I make arrangements.

    That's if nothing untinsels the tree.

For all the trouble we take—the tissue-paper pressing,
the files, the photographs, the boxes stacked away,
the letters—we want more reach.

    Cemeteries tidy up for two generations.

Fear can stretch past noun and verb. Fearly, we fear.
Fearnestly. Fearlorn. Fearest. Fearce. Fearthest. Fearward.
Fear-thee-well.

                              Where are the clock
                              and the angel wings
                              now?

    Tick tick tock. Swirl.

Gratitude

I am thankful for the read-throughs and early input that members of the East Pasadena Monday-night poetry workshop, circa 2013-15, gave to several of the poems: Mary Fitzpatrick, Judith Terzi, Mari L'Esperance, Cathie Sandstrom, Elline Lipkin, and Jenny Factor. Thanks, too, to Genevieve Kaplan, Karen An-hwei Lee, and Mehnaz Sahibzada, who worked on screening for the Tufts Awards in 2016-17 with me and were directly responsible for at least one poem in this book.

My heartfelt appreciation to Adam Deutsch for ushering these poems into print at Cooper Dillon, and to my sister, Elizabeth Dove, for the use of her art on the cover.

Special gratitude for their constancy, their love, and their friendship goes to the animals who share my life, Gus, Fiona, Mae, Wren, and Jesse; to my mother, Louise Dove; to my daughter, Emerson Ellis; and to Angie Vorhies, Judith Terzi, and Scott Larsen.

Linda Dove holds a Ph.D. in Renaissance literature and teaches college writing courses in southern California. Her award-winning books of poetry include her debut collection, *In Defense of Objects* (2009), and the chapbooks, *O Dear Deer,* (2011) and *This Too* (2017), as well as the scholarly collection of essays, *Women, Writing, and the Reproduction of Culture in Tudor and Stuart Britain* (2000). Poems have been nominated for a Pushcart Prize and the Robert H. Winner Award from the Poetry Society of America. Currently, she is serving as the faculty editor for *MORIA*, the national, online literary magazine at Woodbury University. She lives with her human family, plus two Jack Russell terriers and three backyard chickens, in the foothills of Los Angeles.

www.ingramcontent.com/pod-product-compliance
Lightning Source LLC
Chambersburg PA
CBHW030135100526
44591CB00009B/669